MY LOVER IS MINE

MY LOVER IS MINE

WORDS & IMAGES INSPIRED BY THE
ANCIENT LOVE POETRY OF SOLOMON

poetry by

Aly Hawkins & Bryan Ashmore

illustrations and design by

Ramon Deslauriers

Published by Regal Books
From Gospel Light
Ventura, California, U.S.A.
Printed in the U.S.A.

Regal Books is a ministry of Gospel Light, a Christian publisher dedi-
cated to serving the local church. We believe God's vision for Gospel
Light is to provide church leaders with biblical, user-friendly materials
that will help them evangelize, disciple and minister to children, youth
and families. It is our prayer that this Regal book will help you discover
biblical truth for your own life and help you meet the needs of others.
May God richly bless you. For a free catalog of resources from Regal
Books/Gospel Light, please call your Christian supplier or contact us
at 1-800-4-GOSPEL or www.regalbooks.com.

All Scripture quotations are taken from the *KJV—King James Version*.
Authorized King James Version.

To Cerise:

Of all God's creatures, you are without equal.

Authors' Note

We are not scholars.

We are lovers and we are artists.

As lovers, we are devoted to both the here-ness and the transcendence of sexuality expressed in the sacred, mysterious way God intended: with the Other at the heart of the matter, rather than self. And as artists, we seek to express and share our devotion in a way that does justice to that sacred mystery.

There are numerous commentaries on the lush, imagery-laden love poetry found in the book of Song of Songs, and much knowledge and insight can be gleaned from these sources. This volume, however, does not seek to add to that body of knowledge as much as benefit from it. The heart and body experiences of a couple in love 3,000 years ago has much to say to lovers in the twenty-first century. . . they can teach us how to love better and stronger and more deeply if we will only listen awhile to their whispered words.

Let him kiss me with the kisses of his mouth:
for thy love is more delightful than wine.

Song of Solomon 1:2

MY LOVER IS MINE

Let him kiss me with the kisses
of his mouth—

I drink them in,
honeyed wine. . .
the caresses of your lips and teeth and tongue
weaken, strengthen me
I breathe in the scent of your skin,
breathe out the sound of your name

I am willing. . . eager
Lead the way, my lover, my heart
Bring me to your bedchamber—
into the dark
into the light

With my body, I thee worship.

BELOVED

Take me as I am.
I offer scars, imperfections—
touch me and embrace my flaws
I am your beloved
You look at my failings and see
stories
legends, maps of me before
you

I will tell the tales, my lover, only
whisper where I will find you
and I will come out of hiding.
Or we can play cat and mouse. . .
pursuing, escaping
one another until we
collide.
I'll follow your trail and
you follow
mine

BELOVED

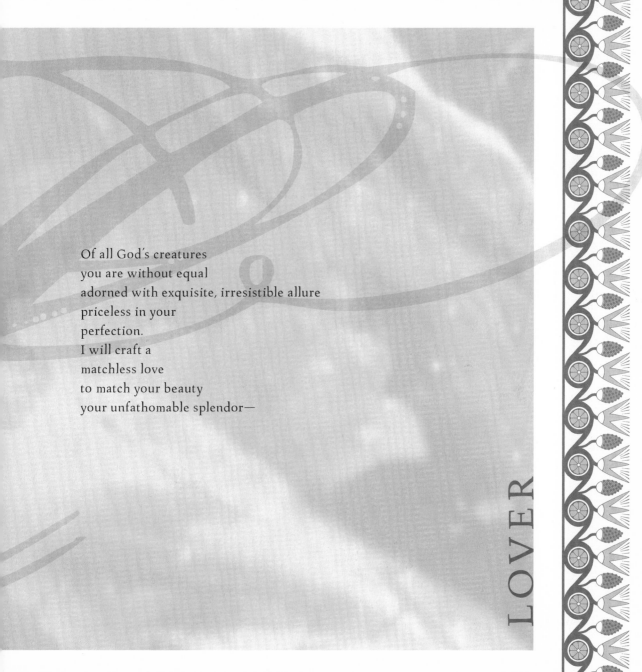

Of all God's creatures
you are without equal
adorned with exquisite, irresistible allure
priceless in your
perfection.
I will craft a
matchless love
to match your beauty
your unfathomable splendor—

LOVER

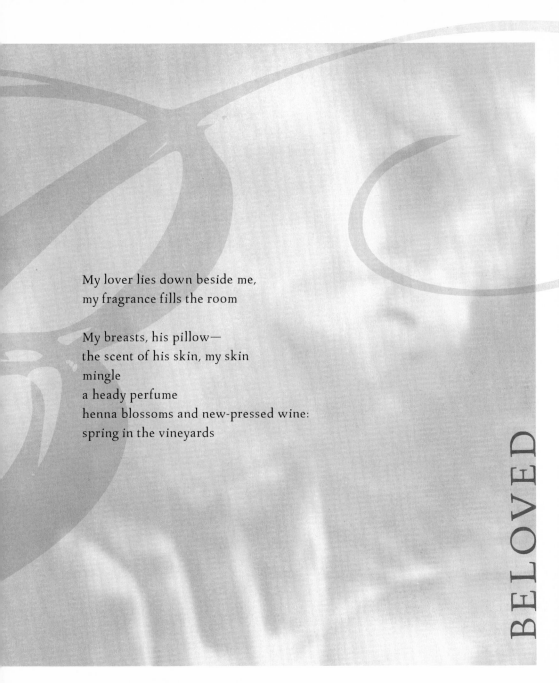

My lover lies down beside me,
my fragrance fills the room

My breasts, his pillow—
the scent of his skin, my skin
mingle
a heady perfume
henna blossoms and new-pressed wine:
spring in the vineyards

BELOVED

I drown in your
peaceful gaze.
Our love will be a shelter
unshakeable
unmoved

LOVER

MI   ND

SO   UL

BO   DY

How persuasive, princely
you are, my lover. . .
your charms entice me
body
mind
soul
The bed we share
shelters us—
safe.

BELOVED

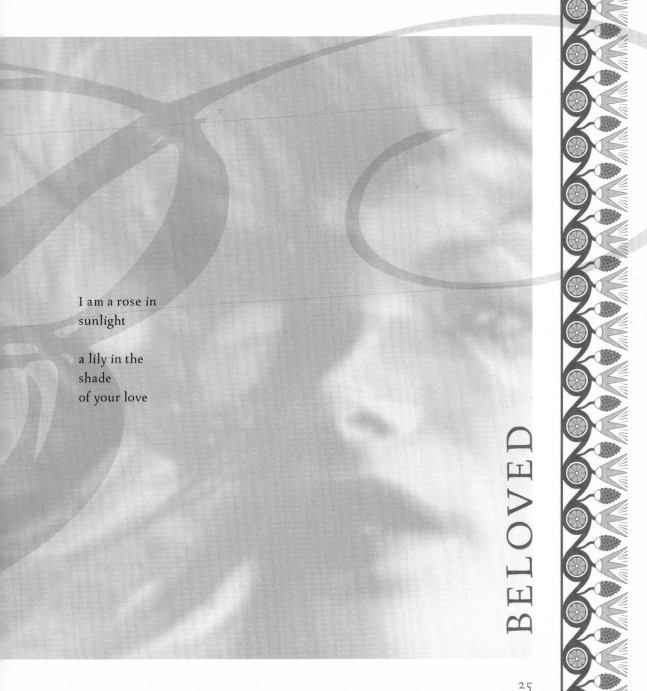

I am a rose in
sunlight

a lily in the
shade
of your love

BELOVED

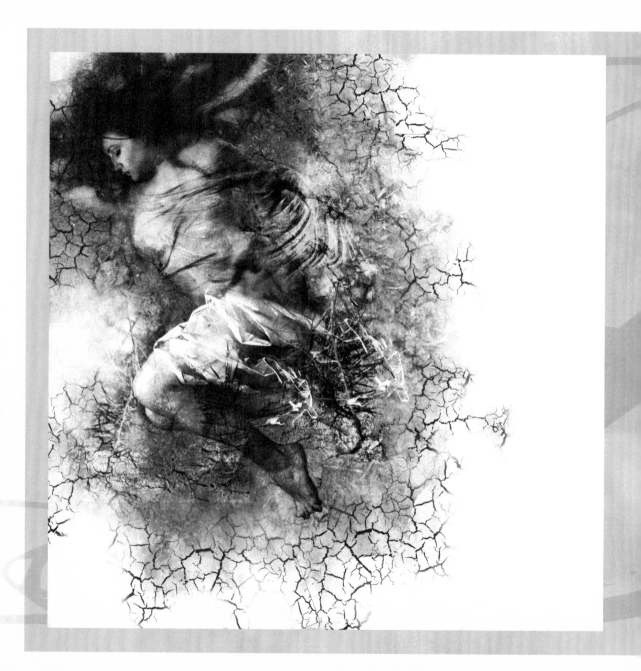

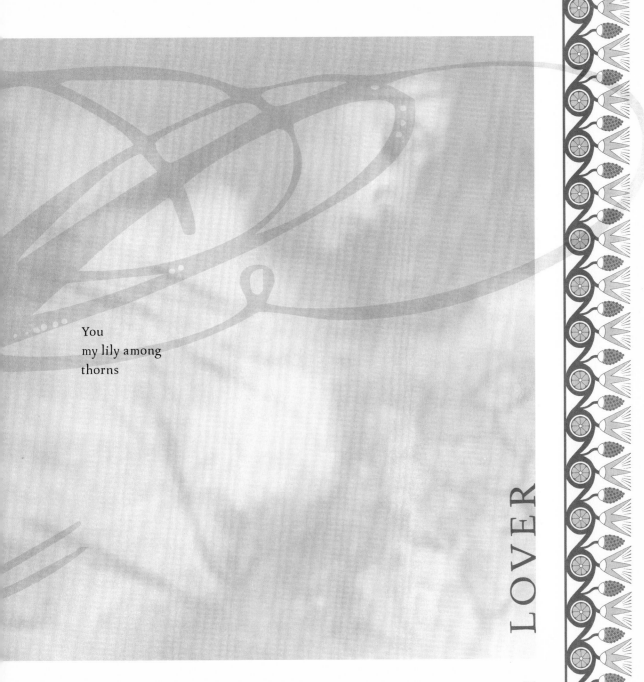

You
my lily among
thorns

LOVER

My lover is a ripe pear tree
in a dark forest of evergreens. . .
let me lie in his shade and taste the tenderness of his fruit
on my tongue

He brings me to the feast
but he's too sated for the banquet to catch his eye
His passion devours me
blazes
scorching sparks
a blind man could see

I should eat something, anything. . .
I need my strength
for what's to come!

BELOVED

In my daydreams, his left arm cradles my head
his right wraps my body around his own

My friends, I beg you by the moon and stars and sun:
do not arouse or awaken love until
its time has come.

BELOVED

Listen!
I hear my lover calling, caressing my name.
Look!
He will cross oceans and deserts and mountains
to lie down at my side

He is unstoppable, like the waves of the sea
beating with relentless desire against
the shores of my resistance
He whispers through the lush tangle of my longing
'til I can resist
no longer

"Come to me."

His breath warm against my neck
"The winter is past—
the slate sky restored to deepest indigo
the bloodless heather replaced by crimson roses
birdsong drowns the crowing of ravens
and we shall have wine from these fragrant vines. . .
but our intoxication
will be desire
Come to me, my beauty.
Come."

BELOVED

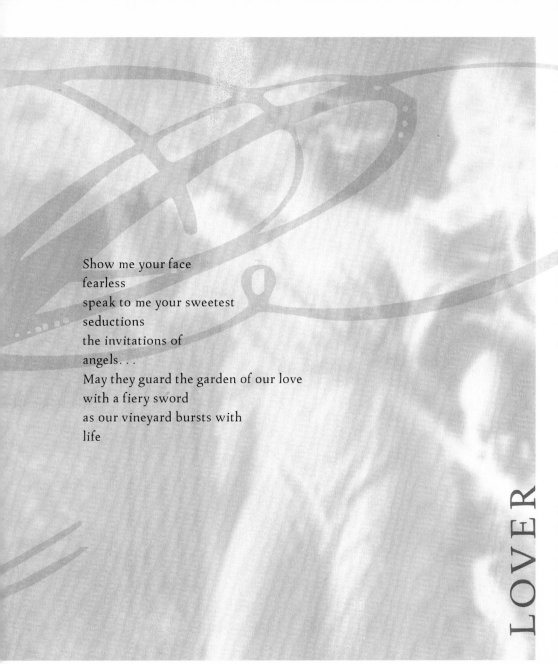

Show me your face
fearless
speak to me your sweetest
seductions
the invitations of
angels. . .
May they guard the garden of our love
with a fiery sword
as our vineyard bursts with
life

LOVER

My lover is mine and
I am his.
My fragrant petals catch his eye,
his breath—
the perfume of my
blossoms
all through the night

When dawn breaks, my lover,
scent of jasmine turns
to dewy roses
dwindling with shadows
to dappled sunlight
Will you turn
to me
in the day,
leaping mountains
to see me in a different light?

BELOVED

37

Restless
sleepless
I lie upon our bed
waiting
longing
for the one my heart loves
He did not come

I must look for him—
the end of the earth is not too far if
he waits for me there

BELOVED

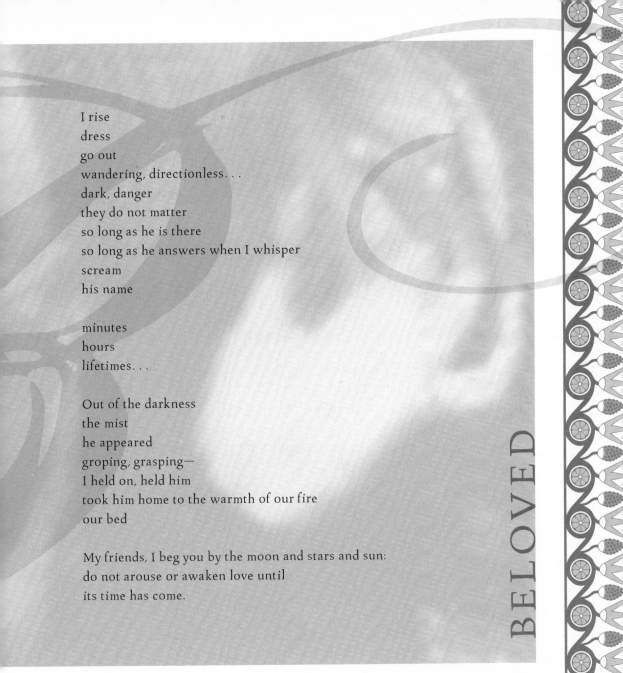

I rise
dress
go out
wandering, directionless. . .
dark, danger
they do not matter
so long as he is there
so long as he answers when I whisper
scream
his name

minutes
hours
lifetimes. . .

Out of the darkness
the mist
he appeared
groping, grasping—
I held on, held him
took him home to the warmth of our fire
our bed

My friends, I beg you by the moon and stars and sun:
do not arouse or awaken love until
its time has come.

BELOVED

Who is this man
to whom I have given my heart, my life?
I know his sweet scent
but I do not know
him

I know his tenderness, gentleness
yet he is a
warrior
ready to do battle for what is his—
sword gleaming
armor shining
chariot fast, furious
inescapable

This, too, is beauty
weighty
grave
A hard beauty carved of iron and stone
diamonds and gold
crowned with purpose
righteousness
goodness
joy

Look upon him
with fear
and
love

BELOVED

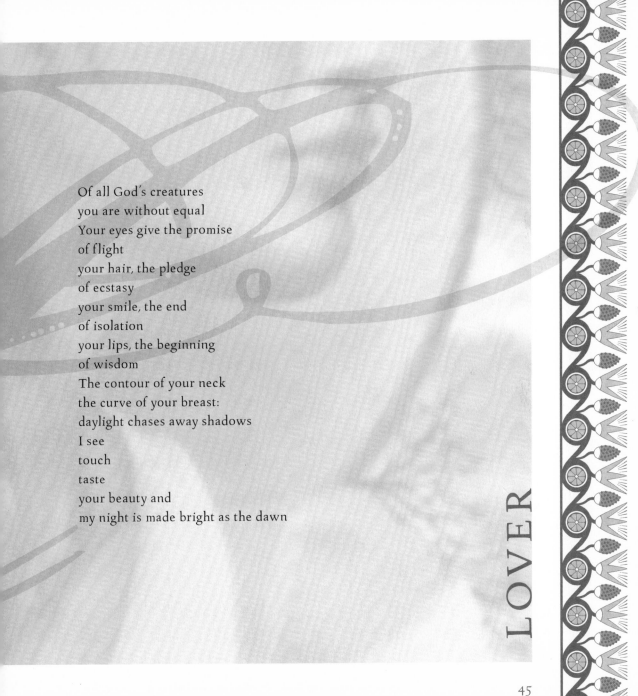

Of all God's creatures
you are without equal
Your eyes give the promise
of flight
your hair, the pledge
of ecstasy
your smile, the end
of isolation
your lips, the beginning
of wisdom
The contour of your neck
the curve of your breast:
daylight chases away shadows
I see
touch
taste
your beauty and
my night is made bright as the dawn

LOVER

Come with me
out of the forest
come with me
into the light
Descend the crest of loneliness
the height of isolation
flee the lion's den
the mountain haunts of predators

You have stolen my heart,
my beloved
my bride
you have stolen my heart
with one glance of
your eyes
with one jewel of
your necklace

LOVER

47

Your love is enchanting
my beloved
more pleasing than wine
the fragrance of your perfume
more than any spice
Your lips drip sweetness
as the honeycomb
my bride
milk and honey
under your tongue
The scent of your garments
like earth
cleansed by rain

LOVER

49

You are a garden locked up
my beloved
my bride
Your body
a spring, fountain,
endless orchard,
your breasts
the choicest of fruits.
I am enveloped in fragrance:
sandalwood and saffron
sage and cinnamon
in aromatic incense and
myrrh and aloes
and scented oil

You are a garden fountain
a well of flowing wetness
drenching the desert of
my tongue

LOVER

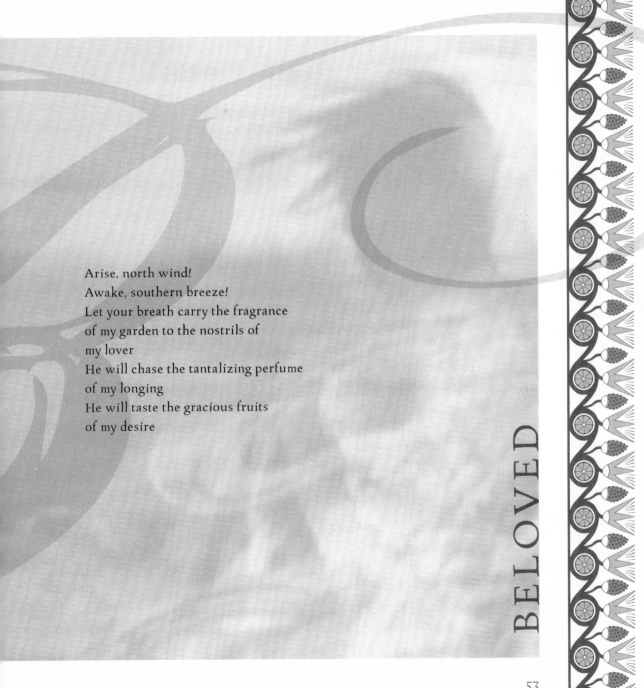

Arise, north wind!
Awake, southern breeze!
Let your breath carry the fragrance
of my garden to the nostrils of
my lover
He will chase the tantalizing perfume
of my longing
He will taste the gracious fruits
of my desire

BELOVED

I steal into your garden
under cover of darkness
Your scent hangs thick in the air
I taste
I breathe
deep, long
you are intoxication
you are nourishment
I drink until
we are
sated

LOVER

I slept
but I dreamed of my lover at the gate
"Open your door, my beloved, my flawless dove.
I am chilled,
drenched with dew and damp
only you can chase away
the cold of night."

I slept
but I dreamed of my lover at the gate
I sang out:
"I have taken off my clothes, I have bathed with scented oils.
Tell me, my lover, my heart. . .
what is it you crave?"
He beat on the gate with frantic desire
My heart hammered in time with his pounding blows
and when I rose from my bed to admit him
my hands and hair and body
dripped
the perfume of longing

BELOVED

I slept
but I dreamed I opened the gate
My lover had vanished into
the mist
I followed him, my heart, into
the vapor
calling, crying his name
No answer

I slept
but I dreamed of the dogs
They hounded me, sniffing out my scent
the aroma of yearning for my lover
was strong
in the cold of night
They bayed with triumph as they brought me
down
Their prey

My friends, I beg you by the moon and stars and sun:
find him
You must
find him and tell him
to wake me
from this nightmare

BELOVED

With the galaxies as my witness,
he outshines
surpasses
exceeds
every lover in the cosmos

I am dazed:

his hair golden dawn in sunlight
and
velvet black in moonshine

his eyes glittering gems in laughter
and
glinting ice in desire

face tender with compassion
and
harsh with need

lips gently coaxing
and
desperately demanding

arms encircling
and
gripping

BELOVED

BELOVED

body inviting
possessing

legs contain
unleash

mouth
soft
rough

all

everything
and in between
my lover

Him

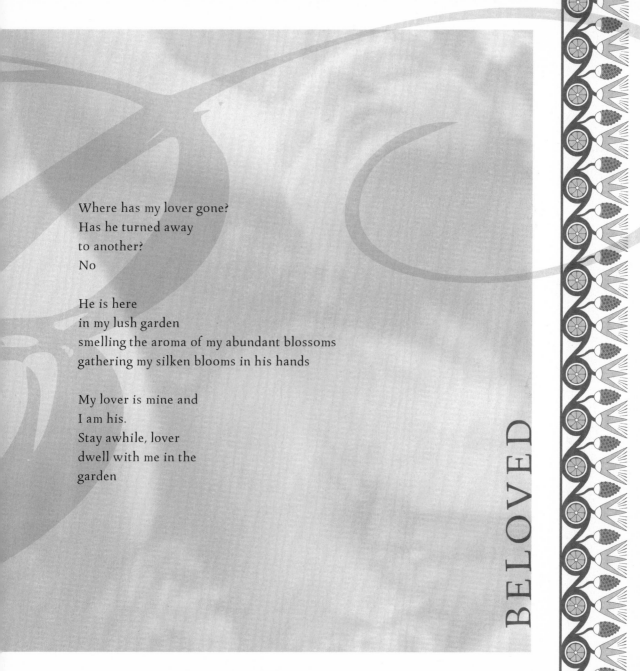

Where has my lover gone?
Has he turned away
to another?
No

He is here
in my lush garden
smelling the aroma of my abundant blossoms
gathering my silken blooms in his hands

My lover is mine and
I am his.
Stay awhile, lover
dwell with me in the
garden

BELOVED

Of all God's creatures
you are without equal
more dazzling than
city lights
more blinding than
a flame in the dark
Your blistering gaze banishes
the shadows
your blazing hair drives out
the night
mouth hypnotizes
face mesmerizes
a single glance
I am conquered

LOVER

Others' charms?
I cannot see
my eyes are blinded by
the singular splendor of
my beloved
my bride
From the moment of her birth
she entranced all who
beheld her
Not one holds a candle
to her beauty
they are reduced to smoldering ashes
in the consuming heat
of her fiery eyes

LOVER

Who is this
rising like the expectant dawn
fair as the full moon
bright as the life-birthing sun
pregnant with meaning
as the stars in portentous procession?

She bears
fruit
the fruit of our passion
I look upon her
and tremble
but my quaking
is stilled by her
quiet gaze

I watch

LOVER

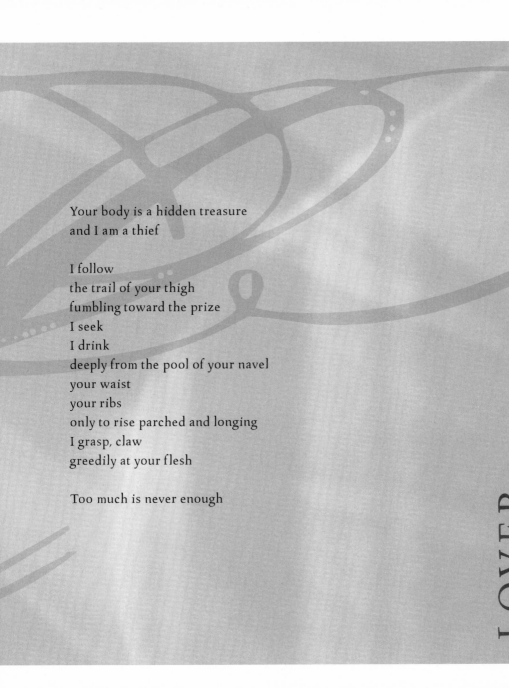

Your body is a hidden treasure
and I am a thief

I follow
the trail of your thigh
fumbling toward the prize
I seek
I drink
deeply from the pool of your navel
your waist
your ribs
only to rise parched and longing
I grasp, claw
greedily at your flesh

Too much is never enough

LOVER

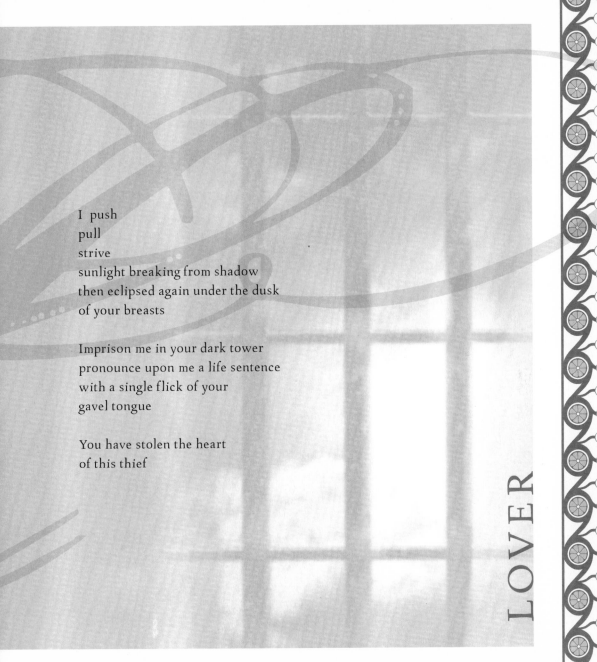

I push
pull
strive
sunlight breaking from shadow
then eclipsed again under the dusk
of your breasts

Imprison me in your dark tower
pronounce upon me a life sentence
with a single flick of your
gavel tongue

You have stolen the heart
of this thief

LOVER

Sip the bouquet of my mouth, my wine
savor it on your lips
your tongue
take it captive
as you captivated
me

Take me away—
away where no one will know us
where no one will notice
when you appraise my vineyards,
full, fragrant with tender fruit
ripe for the tasting
the devouring

BELOVED

We reek of desire.
Our clothes
skin
drip
the smell of night
when we explore familiar terrain:
crook of elbow
blade of shoulder
discover unknown universes:
curve of belly
bone of hip

Stake your claim, lover.

BELOVED

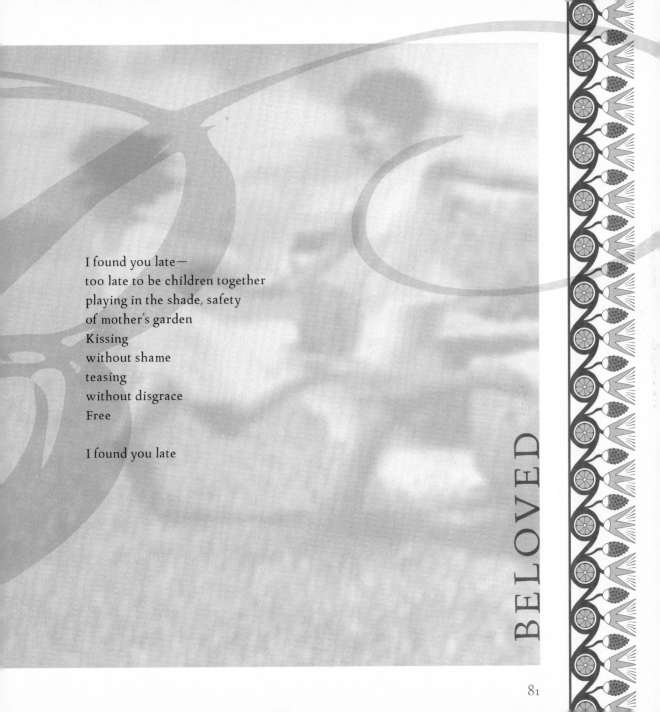

I found you late—
too late to be children together
playing in the shade, safety
of mother's garden
Kissing
without shame
teasing
without disgrace
Free

I found you late

BELOVED

In my daydreams, his left arm cradles my head
his right wraps my body around his own

My friends, I beg you by the moon and stars and sun:
do not arouse or awaken love until
its time has come.

Before my lover:
asleep. . .
parched, dry
desert sands of stinging, pricking
isolation
He roused me:
awake. . .
born again
beneath the pear tree

BELOVED

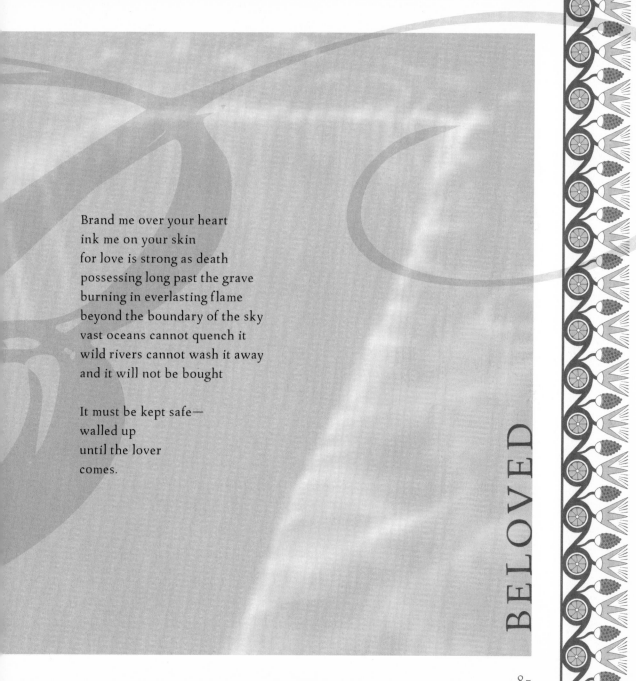

Brand me over your heart
ink me on your skin
for love is strong as death
possessing long past the grave
burning in everlasting flame
beyond the boundary of the sky
vast oceans cannot quench it
wild rivers cannot wash it away
and it will not be bought

It must be kept safe—
walled up
until the lover
comes.

BELOVED

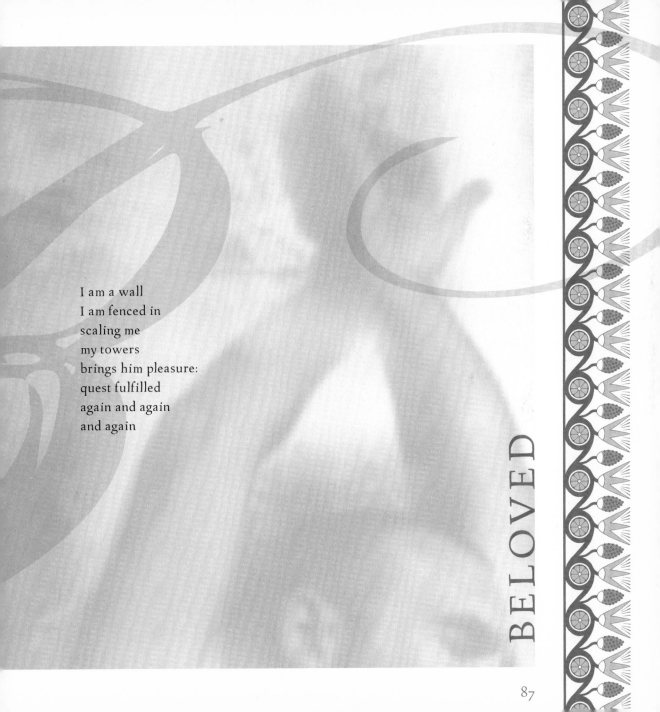

I am a wall
I am fenced in
scaling me
my towers
brings him pleasure:
quest fulfilled
again and again
and again

BELOVED

Lover—
though your fields stretch across the horizon
though your orchards bear fruit for thousands
though you reap the harvest of the world
and sell it for gold and silver beyond counting
nothing shall compare to the
riches I give
freely

BELOVED

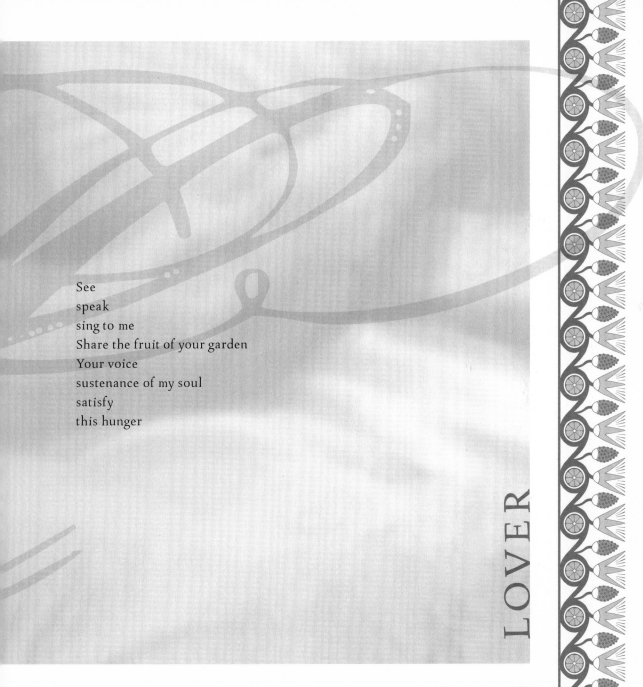

See
speak
sing to me
Share the fruit of your garden
Your voice
sustenance of my soul
satisfy
this hunger

LOVER

Come with me, my lover—
let us ascend
beyond the lofty peaks
soaring

as one

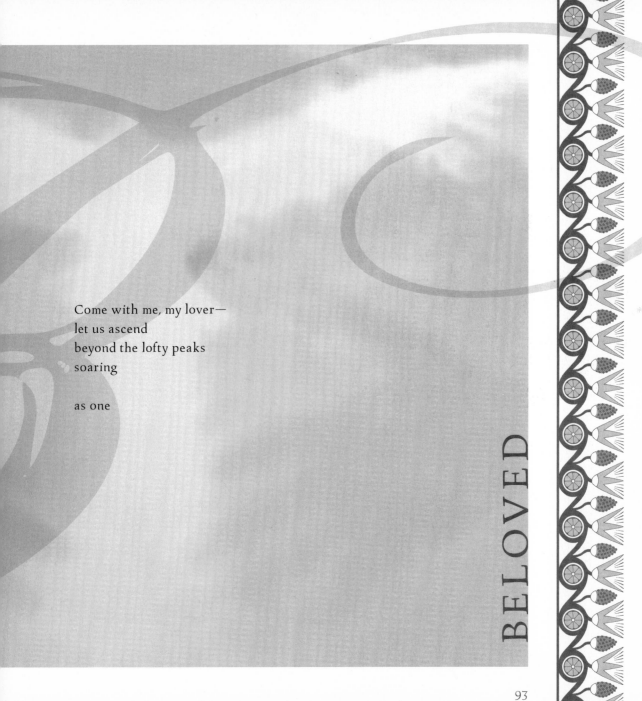